Fiddle Time Joggers

Violin accompaniment book

Kathy and David Blackwell

T0088382

Teacher's note

These duet parts are written to accompany the tunes in *Fiddle Time Joggers*. They are an alternative to the piano accompaniments or audio tracks, and are not designed to be used with those items. With the exceptions of Nos. 4, 43, and 46, these parts may be used with violins playing together with violas (using *Viola Time Joggers* and playing the ensemble parts where appropriate); in a few pieces some details are different between the two books, for example some bar numbers and introductions. A separate viola duet book is available providing duet parts for all the additional tunes in *Viola Time Joggers*.

We are grateful to Simon Stace for all his help in road-testing these duets.

Kathy and David Blackwell

OXFORD
UNIVERSITY PRESS

Great Clarendon Street, Oxford OX2 6DP, England
This collection © Oxford University Press 1998, 2001, 2005, 2013 and 2022
Unless marked otherwise, all pieces (music and words) are by Kathy and David Blackwell and are © Oxford University Press. All traditional pieces are arranged by Kathy and David Blackwell and are © Oxford University Press. Unauthorized arrangement or photocopying of this copyright material is ILLEGAL.

Kathy and David Blackwell have asserted their right under the Copyright, Designs and Patents Act, 1988, to be identified as the Composers of this Work.

ISBN 978-0-19-356200-4

Music and text origination by Katie Johnston
Printed in Great Britain on acid-free paper by
Halstan & Co. Ltd, Amersham, Bucks.

Contents

1. Bow down, O Belinda 3
2. Under arrest! 3
3. Someone plucks, someone bows 4
4. Down up 4
5. Two in a boat 5
6. London Bridge 5
7. Fast lane 6
8. In flight 7
9. Lift off! 8
10. Katie's waltz 8
11. Copy cat 9
12. Tap dancer 10
13. Rhythm fever 11
14. Here it comes! 12
15. So there! 12
16. Rowing boat 13
17. Ally bally 14
18. Tiptoe, boo! 14
19. Travellin' slow 16
20. Lazy cowboy 16
21. Off to Paris 17
22. Clare's song 18
23. City lights 19
24. The three friends 20
25. Peace garden 20
26. Summer sun 22
27. Phoebe in her petticoat 23
28. Ready, steady, go now! 23
29. Cooking in the kitchen 24
30. Happy go lucky 24
31. The mocking bird 26
32. Algy met a bear 26
33. Listen to the rhythm 27
34. Cattle ranch blues 28
35. In the groove 29
36. Stamping dance 30
37. Distant bells 30
38. Lazy scale 31
39. The old castle 32
40. Rocking horse 33
41. Patrick's reel 34
42. Calypso time 35
43. Knock, knock! 36
44. Rocky mountain 36
45. Carrion crow 37
46. Flying high 38
47. Fiddle Time 39

1. Bow down, O Belinda

American folk tune

2. Under arrest!

KB & DB

Say the word '*rest*' quietly to yourself as you play.

3. Someone plucks, someone bows

Traditional
Words KB & DB

4. Down up

KB & DB

* Fill in the letter names of these notes.

5. Two in a boat

American folk tune

6. London Bridge

English folk tune

7. Fast lane

Try even faster the second time through!

8. In flight

KB & DB

In the rests, let your bow make a circle as you swoop and soar like a bird.

9. Lift off!

KB & DB

Lift your bow off in each of the rests and let it orbit! (Make a circle with your right arm.)

10. Katie's waltz

KB & DB

11. Copy cat

KB & DB

12. Tap dancer

KB & DB

* Hold the bow upright and tap the screw end of the bow on your music stand.

13. Rhythm fever

KB & DB

14. Here it comes!

KB & DB

* Think of a foody rhythm and play it on these notes.

15. So there!

KB & DB

16. Rowing boat

KB & DB

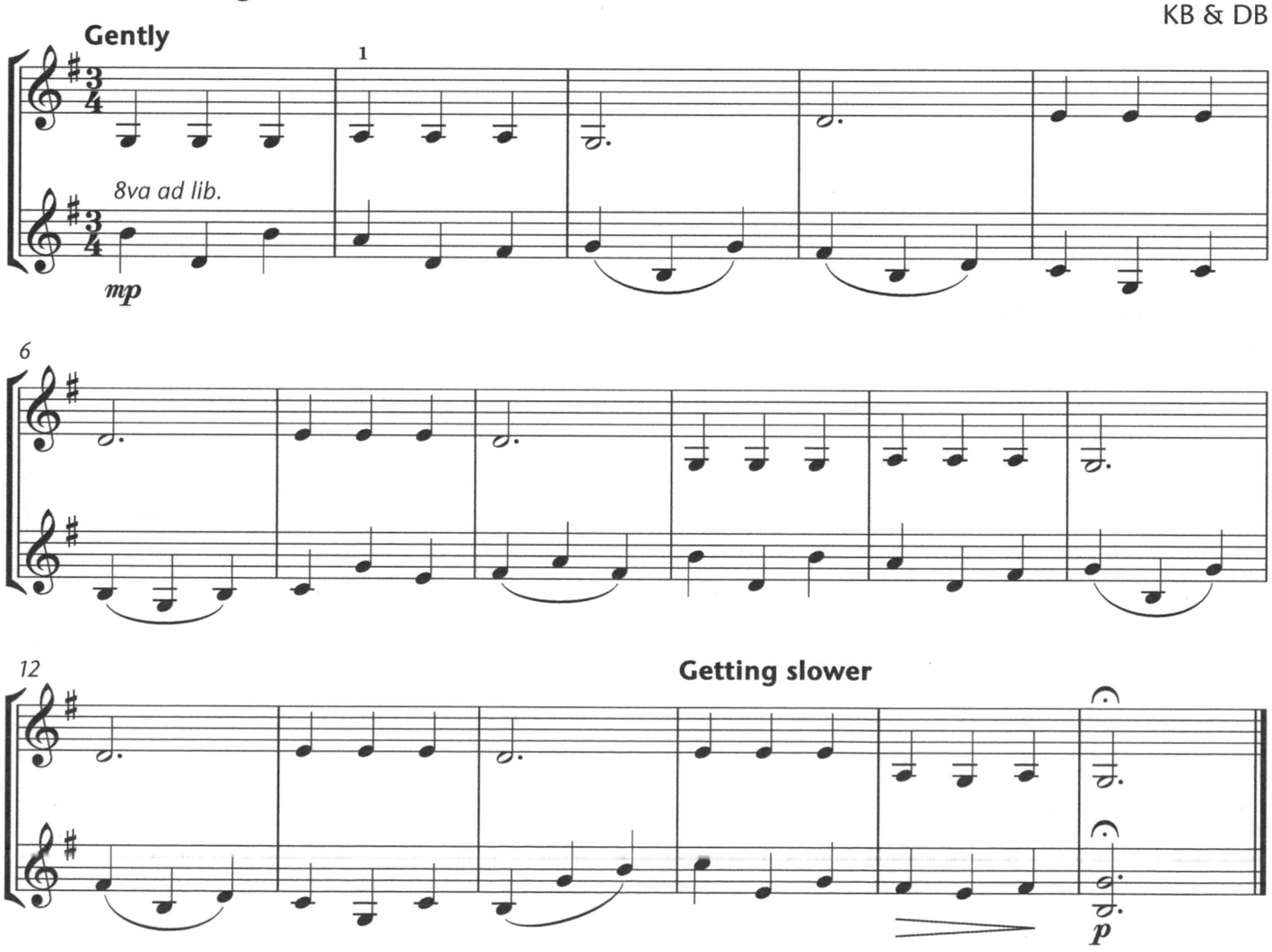

17. Ally bally

Scottish folk tune

18. Tiptoe, boo!

KB & DB

The pupil's part may also be played pizzicato.

19. Travellin' slow

KB & DB

20. Lazy cowboy

KB & DB

21. Off to Paris

French folk tune

22. Clare's song

KB & DB

23. City lights

KB & DB

24. The three friends

Finnish folk tune

25. Peace garden

KB & DB

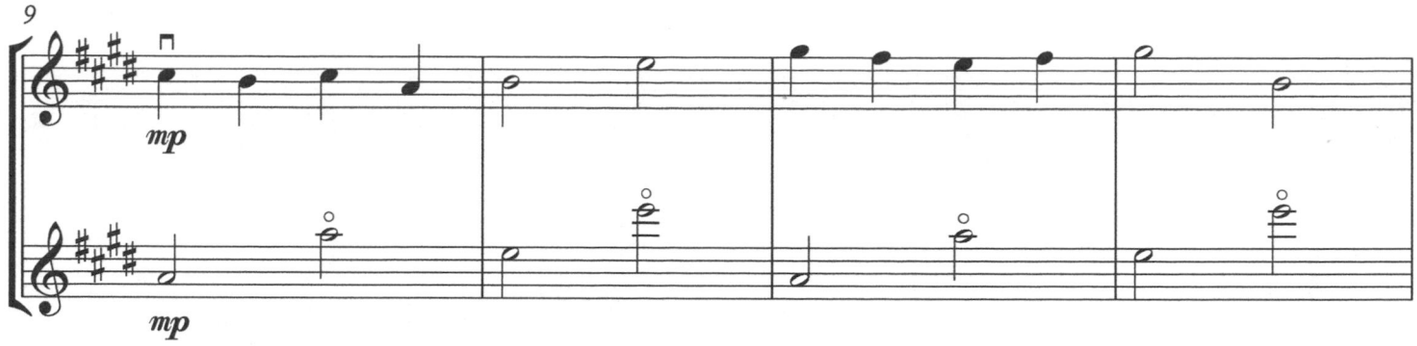
9
mp
mp

13

17
f
f

21
ff

26. Summer sun

KB & DB

27. Phoebe in her petticoat

American folk tune

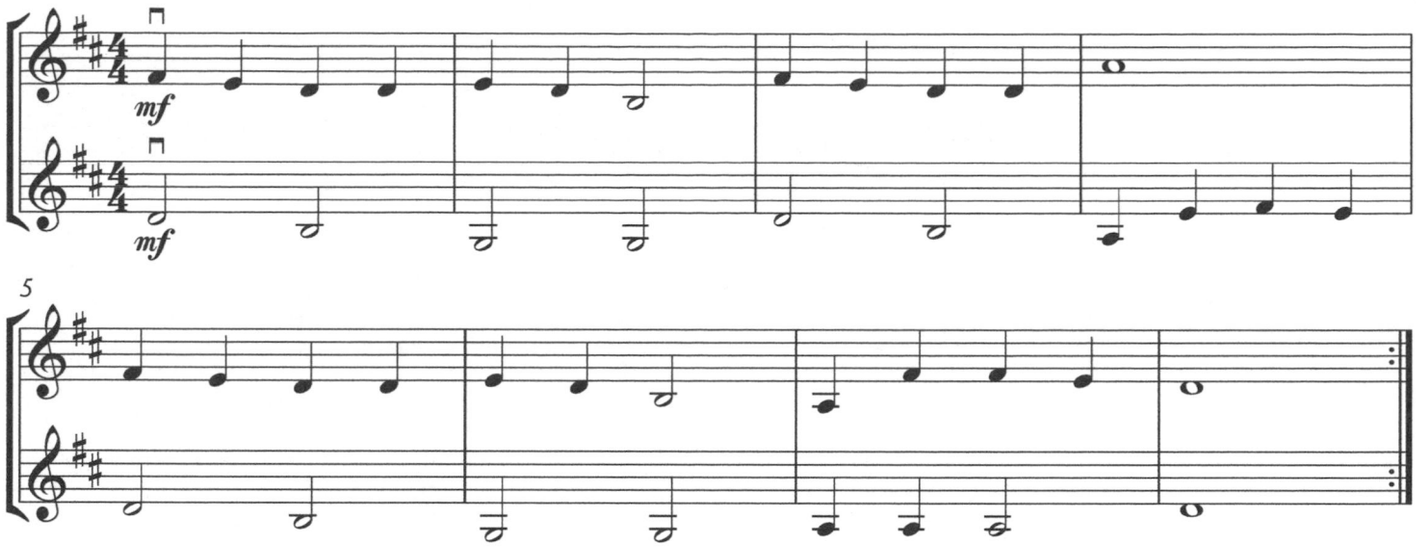

Swap parts when you do the repeat.

28. Ready, steady, go now!

KB & DB

29. Cooking in the kitchen

KB & DB

30. Happy go lucky (for Iain)

KB & DB

13
mf
mf
19
f
f
25
31
ff
ff

31. The mocking bird

American folk tune

32. Algy met a bear

KB & DB
Words anon.

Swap parts when you do the repeat.

33. Listen to the rhythm

KB & DB

34. Cattle ranch blues

KB & DB

35. In the groove

KB & DB

36. Stamping dance

Czech folk tune

37. Distant bells

KB & DB

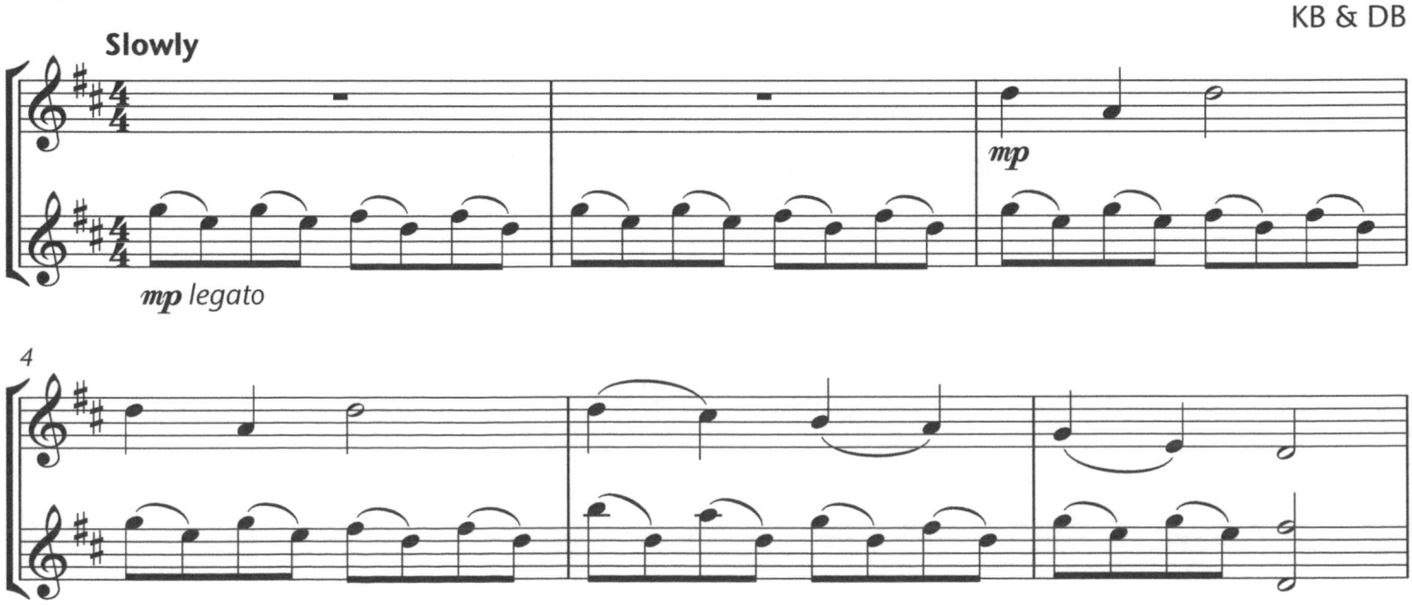

38. Lazy scale

KB & DB

39. The old castle

With a singing tone

KB & DB

40. Rocking horse

KB & DB

41. Patrick's reel

KB & DB

42. Calypso time

KB & DB

43. Knock, knock!

Make up some other 'Knock, knock' jokes and play them on your violin.

44. Rocky mountain

45. Carrion crow

American folk tune

46. Flying high

KB & DB

47. Fiddle Time

KB & DB